I0756300

FINISHING LINE PRESS
www.finishinglinepress.com

Emerald Echoes

poems by

Dorothy Doyle

Finishing Line Press
Georgetown, Kentucky

Emerald Echoes

To my ancestors, whose sacrifices and resilience
will always inspire me.
Míle buíochas le grá.
(A thousand thanks, with love.)

ISBN 979-8-89990-490-5 First Edition

Publisher: Leah Huete de Maines
Editor: Christen Kincaid
Cover Art: Dr. Niamh Hamill
Author Photo: Ryan P. Doyle
Cover Design: Elizabeth Maines McCleavy

Order online: www.finishinglinepress.com
also available on amazon.com

Author inquiries and mail orders:
Finishing Line Press
PO Box 1626
Georgetown, Kentucky 40324
USA

Contents

Quarantine Athchuairt

Ireland, 1847

She was sick with famine fever and could not keep up.
—Eavan Boland, "Quarantine"

As we trudge along the rocky boreen,
west and west and north,
to the HMS Elizabeth that waits in Killala Bay,
you beg me to keep walking.

Your hand clutches mine so tight
I fear my fingers will crack in its grip—
but you croon sweet words, "just a bit more,
acushla, we are bound for America in the morning..."

and I move as well as I can,
but the rags you bound to my feet
have ripped open to the ground
and I feel my blood ooze

as it leaves crimson footprints in our wake,
and I must rest.

Mary Magdalene in Pigtails
Long Island, 1961

I sit cross-legged
on the dusty wood floor
of your closet
the smell of mothballs and shoe polish
overpowered by the warm aroma
of potatoes and pot roast
baking downstairs.
Through the closed bedroom door
I hear you sing a duet
with Patsy Kline as she
croons heartbreak
on the radio.

A cat burglar in pink pajamas,
I paw through the frayed pockets
of faded house dresses,
searching for pieces of you.
A broken rosary.
A hairpin.
A faded Mass card
with the Blessed Mother on the front,
an Irish blessing on the back.

The mink stole you inherited from Aunt Mary
nibbles my shoulder,
its teeth bared in an eternal grimace,
dead eyes fixed on mine.
The afternoon sun peeks through
the venetian blinds casting a dust filled
spotlight on your red patent leather heels.

Those scarlet shoes, a siren's song,
beckon my prepubescent soul.
I sashay across your room,
flip my hair, and pout my lips
as I click-clack

across the rugless floor,
my hips swaying to the imaginary beat.

I am Mhaighdean Mhara,
a selkie in swimmies,
Mary Magdalene in pigtails,
Delilah wielding safety scissors—
a flat chested temptress
in flowered footy pajamas
and a Minnie Mouse bathrobe.

Daddy Issues

Lingering whiffs of smoke and sweat
cling to the fabric of the hastily hung tweed jacket.
She holds a sleeve close to her face and breathes in
scents of city streets and subway cars.
Small hands search frayed pockets
seeking fragments of his day—
a ticket stub from the Long Island Railroad
a stick of Juicy Fruit gum
a cigarette butt.
The Unholy Artifacts of a distant father.
She hides them in her overall pockets.

Searching for him in the quiet house
she hears Lady Day croon
"lonely is the laundry you don't have to hide,"
on the old Philco radio he bought from an army buddy.
Smoke obscures his face.
He sits in his corner chair,
the glowing tip of a Chesterfield the only light in the room.
She watches quietly from behind the half-closed door.
Her fingers caress the precious relics
hidden in her overall pockets.

Saintly Aspirations

Evening prayers prayed.
Good night kisses kissed.
The antiphonal duet
of parental snores
at last cascades
down the darkened hallway.

On my bedside table, a worn copy
of *The Divine Lives and Glorious Deaths of the Saints*
lies cloistered under a stack of Nancy Drew books—
my nightly foray into aspirational sainthood.
Inside, paintings of martyrs at the moment
of gruesome death, smiling beatifically,
eyes bulged heavenward as arrows pierce their necks
and tongues of flame nip their feet.

St Dymphna, patron saint for those of us with
nervous afflictions
        (to whom my mother prayed daily.)
St Agnes, patron of the loved and abused.
St Cecilia, patron saint of poets,
first confidante and mentor.

First Awakening

Then the eyes of both were opened,
and they knew that they were naked.
—Genesis 3:7

My mother would bathe
my sister and me in one tub—
maybe to save water,
maybe to save time.
She'd leave us to soak,
the water cooling around us
as we giggled and squealed,
blowing shampoo bubbles and
shaping our hair into mohawks
and Elvis pompadours.

One Sunday
Ginny and I poured water
over each other's heads
until floors were soaked
and fingers crinkled.
As usual, Ginny started crying
"Soap is stinging my eyes!"

With the shriek of a banshee
Mother flew in
with a "Stop your whinjin now!'"
her brogue thick as cream,
rubbing us down briskly
with starched white towels
until our pale skin turned pink
and a cacophonic squall
of cries, squeals, and
"Jesus, Mary, and Josephs!"
filled the bathroom.
Finally, with a quick smack on the rear,
she sent us out in the hallway naked.

Seated in a corner chair
a man—
an uncle—
with narrow eyes
that followed
like a Leonardo painting—
looking keenly at
the two alabaster bodies—
and though just six,
my eyes opened wide,
and I felt
naked,
appraised,
ashamed.

For Ginny

Exuberant rosebud,
unannounced usurper,
you landed by my side
without asking permission.
All violet-eyed and raven-curled—
pink bouquets of Dad's
springtime azaleas
bloomed on your baby cheeks.
Next to you I wilted,
a skittish clinging vine,
pale, thin,
quiet, shy.
I kept thinking that,
like an overdue book
or a bad carton of eggs,
they'd return you.
But you stayed and grew,
a mischievous, charming
thief in the light,
who took my dolls,
wore my clothes,
stole my mom.
In a room with
lavender curtains
and pink lampshades
we shared a bunkbed,
me on top by the crucifix,
you on the bottom,
by the clock radio.
I was the smart one.
You were the funny one.
I was the skinny one.
You were the chubby one,
each growing up believing
that the other had what was needed
to feel whole.

An Ode to Sister Mary Catherine

I named my dog after you,
Sister Mary Catherine.
She's black, like the habit which rustled
along the floor and left a trailing cloud
of dust bunnies in your wake.
You always tucked your hands
beneath the bodice.
Is that where you kept
your secret stash of rubber bands
ready to snap at the kids
who messed up the times tables?
I'd watch the veins in your neck in horror
as they throbbed all red and bulging
when you'd grab Jimmy Cavanaugh by the ear
for snickering during the Sorrowful Mysteries.
We all waited for the wimple to blast off your head
to see if Tommy Healy was right
when he said you were bald underneath those heavy veils.

Now I wonder if, like my canine
Mary Catherine, who gets cranky
when tired, and I dress her like a nun,
you were just in need of a loving pat
and a whisper in your unwrenched ear—
"You are *such a precious girl.*"

Co-conspirators

Pinky lifted, which always makes me laugh,
his arthritic hand shakes as he holds
the whiskey glass to parched, anticipating lips.
Tell me dad, where did a kid from
the tenements of Brooklyn
learn to hold his pinky up—just so—like
Upper East Side ladies at afternoon tea?
With a triumphant thump he plants
that drained tumbler on the counter,
then tap-taps the rim with his arched aristocratic digit.

The warden's orthopedic Keds
squeak warning on the wooden floor outside the kitchen
as I pour a shot—
acknowledged with a wink—
emptied in a flash
(professional that he is),
pinky raised—(gentleman that he is),
before her sneakered feet cross the threshold.

Thanks, Mom

New Jersey, 2025

Like a medieval nun,
you consumed your days in communion with God,
self-denial your signature landscape of self-flagellation,
but for the nightly indulgence of chocolate squares
you hid in the drawer under the dish towels.

I'd watch you rinse dishes after supper,
lips silent in perpetual devotion,
the swishing bubbles your baptismal soundtrack.

I inherited your inherent anxiety
without the benefit of your piety.

At the sink I try to drown the past
with Madonna's "Like a Prayer,"
then devour broken pieces of Debauve & Gallais
stashed in my drawer under your frayed dish towels.

Harvest

for my father

Like the bog woman unburied from a grave of peat,
still clad in the cloak in which she died,
you sublimated the suffering of ancient generations
beneath the plaid woolen jacket you wore every autumn
to prepare your garden for winter's frost.

So many late Septembers, as air bled cool from the bay
I'd watch you dig shallow graves
for your precious hyacinth bulbs.
You lifted them to the sky like communion hosts
then tucked them in under blankets of compost
made from summer's leftover suppers.

I stood by your side, a small watchful companion—
told to look but never to touch as I learned their names
hyacinthus orientalus and *transcaspicus,*
until you buried me too in this garden of grief
where I flourished, nourished by silence
and darkness, until I emerged tall and strong—
custodian of the secrets I carry
beneath a plaid woolen jacket as I walk
through fragrant beds of lavender hyacinth.

The Worst Hour

In the worst hour of the worst season
Of the worst year of a whole people
—Eavan Boland "Quarantine"

My sweet acushla died today
As I held her to my breasts long dry,
While hunger held its ghostly sway
And on God's mercy we relied.

As I held her to my breasts long dry,
We prayed God spare us one more day,
For on God's mercy we relied
As hunger held its ghostly sway.

We prayed God spare us one more day
Our cabin grew cold as the fire died,
The hunger held its ghostly sway
It was on God's mercy we relied.

Our cabin grew cold as the fire died
I held her to my breasts long dry
God has no mercy I realized
And I longed once more to hear her cry.

I held her to my breasts long dry
As ghostly hunger held its sway
I longed once more to hear her cry
My sweet acushla died today.

Steerage

Kingstown Port, Dublin, June 1855

Survivors
scale swaying gangways in silence
until the coffin ship
swallows them
into its pitch black belly.
Down into steerage they carry
bulging muslin sacks thick with threadbare linens,
tattered prayer books, a hand-sewn doll,
a pair of shabby boots.

On the pier, a young mother
clings to her swaddled baby
as the ship's horn blasts a final warning.
She passes the child to an old woman
who waits by a wagon and whispers,
"Slán, mo chuisle."
"Slán agat."
"I will send for you soon."

Eiderdown Dreams

July 1855

The heaving ship tossed soaking swells
of mist and misery on all of us hunkered below,
causing some to wish,
between their Hail Marys and Glory Bes,
they had never left behind our heartbroken land.

The sick quarantined,
confined to quarters,
John Joe and I held fast to one another
beneath eiderdown blankets still soft with the scent
of the meadowsweet you plucked fresh
from the hedgerow outside your bedroom window
the morning we bid you goodbye.

September 1855

New York City

Dear Mam,

Mam please, if you would,
say a prayer of thanksgiving
to the blessed St Christopher,
who guided our journey
across the great ocean
for we've arrived safely
on America's shore.

John Joe says he's surprised
that the streets of New York
are not paved to the brim
with bright carats of gold
and fresh mint dollar bills,
but instead with manure,
and puddles of mud
that splash and spray slop
on his new shoes and socks.

By brother Pat's house
we passed a dead pig
in the middle of Perry Street,
down by the quay.
Flies buzzed round its face
while a volcano of maggots
oozed in the entrails
of its bloated pink belly.

In New York's sooty air
they hang clothes out to dry
on ropes that crisscross
over open courtyards.
From our window I see
John Joe's handsome wool knickers
as they dance in the wind

with our neighbor's pink nightgown
like they're flirting and laughing
at O'Donovan's Pub.

Mam, how I long for a stroll
on the windswept boreen
that runs by our cottage
and down to the sea,
and the sweet scent
of freshly washed bedsheets and towels
as they hang in the breezes
beyond the dry stone walls.

Late Fall, 1855

Ballyragget, Kilkenny

Dear Bridget,

The hedgerows in the lane
are turning fast to the colors of fall.
End of summer's fading plumes—
sweetbriar and primrose hang low on the fence,
their leaf-bare stems waving welcome
to the green-brown bracken
and rust-colored mums
that line the path your footsteps
once ran to our cottage door.
Soon winter will be upon us.
I will stock the feeder hung by the garden gate
with brown berries and the sunflower seeds
Mrs Leary brought when she came last Tuesday for tea.
I hope to lure some siskins and starlings
to the oak tree by the window
to trill their songs and parade their bright colors
through the winter's still, dusty mornings.

November 1855

New York City

A faded gray horse lies dead
in the street outside the front window,
his rotting carcass the same dull color
as the sky above the bare trees.
Cool breezes off the Hudson
billow the once white lace curtains
you sent for Christmas
and blow the poor beast's stench
into our front room
where I sit in the dark
beside the sleeping wee one
and wait for the sound of John Joe's footsteps
by the front door.

December 1855

Ballyragget, Kilkenny

Dear Bridget,

The braying of your old nag Tadhg
did give me quite a start.
I was peeling boiled potatoes
for your father's evening meal.
I turned around in time to see
his dappled shaggy snout
squeeze through the opened window jamb
to steal an uninvited bite
of the freshly baked soda bread
I had cooling on the sill.
Dad's dog Fergus barked in fury
and the baby laughed and laughed
as I grabbed the broom from
o'er the hearth
and swung and swept
and swept and swung
that whuffling,
braying black hooved thief
back out into the night.

If I could Brid, I swear I would
I'd buy that divil a one-way fare
on the next ship out of Liverpool
to go and live with you and John
on the cobbled streets of New York.

Mam

January 1856
Ballyragget, Kilkenny

Dear Bridget,

I heard the banshee's wail again
among the trees down in the glen.
I turned with a start and didn't I see
your father, back curved low,
over the turf fire, tending to our pot of stew.
He is now so bent and frail with age
my own breath comes short each time
I hear the banshee's howl.

Michael, love, I'm off to pick
the last of summer's peas.
Wait in the soft wee chair.
Warm your feet by the fire.
I won't be gone but a moment or so.

I ran past the garden and up the hill
to Mother Mary's holy well
where the friar hid the chalice
from the Sassenach soldiers long ago.
There the mighty oak grew tall
from the blood that streamed hot
from the soldiers' blades upon his neck.

I tied a blue bow to the giant oak's branch,
said a quick prayer, and ran back to the house.
Your Da's boots like soldiers upright and proud
side by side on the hearth by the roaring turf fire,
but his stockinged feet lay quiet on the cold cabin floor,
as still as the gravestones in St Brigid's church yard.

As I bent close to say goodbye,
the turf fire flicked kisses
across your father's face,
gray now, like the sea holly
we picked last summer by the strand.

March 1856

Ballyragget, Kilkenny

Wait for Me

At midnight, Michael,
the taibhse swirl
in firelight shadows
on the clay walls of the cottage.
They encircle me,
as if to entice me to join them
in their hastening dance.
I hear the banshees
call my name on the March wind
that shoots down the chimney.
The turf ashes twirl
like whispering sirens
luring me to death.

Cecilia

New York City, 1926

Six kids asleep down the hall
three to a bed, head to feet.
She holds the baby tight under the covers,
and prays to the Blessed Mother
no staggering footfalls
will fill the home tonight.

Veronica

New York, 1926

I stand on tiptoes
in my new Easter shoes
to get a better look at
Eddie asleep in the box
that lies in the middle of the parlor.
His face is white, like the chalk
we use to play hopscotch
on the sidewalk downstairs.
Grandpa's old red rosary beads
are wrapped like ribbons
around his fingers.
Grandma says she heard a
banshee keening by her window
the night they took him away.
And now he's back—
lying still in a box.
All the mirrors are covered—
All the windows are open—
Grandma says his soul needs to go.
Mama is crying in the kitchen.
Papa is silent in his chair.
Grandma is praying her rosary.
And I'm climbing into the box
with my brother to keep him
from leaving me.

Veronica

New York, 1931

Pop lets out a low moan
as I tiptoe past him—
passed out on the parlor floor
between a knocked-over crucifix and an empty bottle of Jameson.

Mama is on the phone,
her voice low,
her face red with shame.
She sees me and hangs up quickly.
"Don't forget your lunch, love,"
as if there is not a
person lying drunk—
on the floor—
between
us.

Cecilia

New York, 1933

The mother's veined hands gnarled with age
grip the sleeping daughter's
graying fingers that cool too quickly
on the starched white bedsheets,
as if to tether her to the earth
for just a bit longer.

A medical machine, like a metronome,
keeps time with the last jagged breaths
and the muffled sobs of children
gathered like puffins around her bed.

The priest makes the sign of the cross
on her forehead with warm holy oil
and glances at the husband,
who is silent as a shadow in the doorway,
his hat in his hand, whiskey on his breath,
until he staggers out the apartment door and
into the comforting clamor of Columbus Avenue.

Immigrant Lament

She sits in silence
as the slanted light
sifts through dusty windows
and the bustling city
winds down for the day.
The rocker in the corner
has become her chapel,
her confessional,
her mourning chair.
Sorrows kaleidoscope
the whisky glass she cradles
still holding fast to her rosary beads.
Her mind spins and falls back
on the leafy hills of Connemara,
to the shaming nuns of Tuam,
and the child who will never know
her heartbroken Máthair.

Shared Sustenance

Donegal, 2025

Through fairy tree branches
slung low with weight of soggy rags and prayers
I watched,
as with cupped hands, one by one,
they partook of the holy well
as its water trickled down the hill to Abbey Bay.
Silhouetted by the sun as it rose over dusky Sligo mountains,
they egged one another on with laughter and chatter.
Curious, I turned to trace the water up through the thicket
and saw a grey ewe standing, newborn lamb by her side,
as she watched them drink the runoff of the stream
she and her flock were wading through
to wash down the grass and silage of their morning meals.

Seanmáthair in Spring

In the morning, like the Cailleach,
she carries stones in her pockets
to mark her return through woods
where dogs chase squirrels
and newborn rabbits peek from fur-lined nests,
their noses blush pink as the ripening
nipple buds that trumpet from tree limbs
to give warning that the warming sun
will soon abide and she will descend,
once again, under spring's softening ground
wearing her black woolen shawl,
tattered stockings, and worn-out leather shoes.

St Patrick's Day on the Auld Sod, Donegal, 2025

Had I the heavens' embroidered cloths
Enwrought with golden and silver light
—W.B. Yeats

Triskelion swirls upon our cheeks,
we walked arm in arm in the emerald-embroidered cloths
and crocheted caps of the women of Cumann na mBan.
Our black-laced shoes kept pace with the whines and thunder
of Bundoran's Pipes and Drums and strode past throngs
who held the Tricolour high and held the hands of kids
who smiled and waved as we walked by.

A stranger in a strange land,
yet I felt the pipes and drums
hammer ripples through my soles—
the agony of my unplanted ancestors.

C Train to Chambers Street

An apparition in a tracksuit,
small brown feet in scuffed sandals,
she makes her way through the crowd
of St Patrick's Day revelers,
a baby boy papoosed to her chest,
a pigtailed toddler in hand-me-downs
whining in her wake.

As we tunnel underground
she offers packs of Skittles and Kit Kats
to riders suddenly entranced
with overhead ads for Dr. Zizmor, Dermatologist,
and *Les Misérables*, the musical.

Three generations past starvation
we have forgotten the million
who perished in rotting fields,
in disease ridden workhouses,
and Trevelyan's cruel words
that their suffering was God's will,
divine and just punishment
for their rebellious, indolent ways.

Notes

"Quarantine Athchuairt": Athchuairt (Irish) translates as "revisited" and "boreen" (Irish) as country road.

"Seanmáthair in Spring": Cailleach is a powerful, mythological Celtic old woman, associated with winter and the Irish landscape.

With Thanks

With love and gratitude:
To my parents Veronica and James Teevan, who inherited this legacy before me.
To my brothers and sisters Jimmy, Ronald, Veronica, Patsy, and Ginny, who share this legacy with me.
To my son Ryan, daughter Cáitlin, and daughter in law Kathleen, to whom the legacy has been passed. I dedicate these poems to you.

Special thanks and love:
To Nan Bryan, my original mentor, who first inspired my love of poetry.
To my fellows, John, Melissa, Tony, Charlotte, Zafira, Sarah, Niki, Morgan, and Bree, for your honesty and support, but most of all for all the laughs.
To Michael Waters, the kindest and most honest second reader one could ever ask for.
To Michaela Moscaliuc, who patiently nurtured this nervous neophyte and gave me the confidence to believe that even in the eighth decade of life I might have something to say. I learned so much from you.

Last but not least:
To my husband Mark, with all my love, who recognized our common legacy from the moment we met in an elevator at 44 Wall Street, forty-seven years ago.

Dorothy Doyle returned to graduate school at the beginning of Covid at the age of 66. Over the course of the subsequent five years, she completed a Master's in English followed by an MFA in Creative Writing. Her short story "A Response to Prozac Nation: A Mother's Perspective" received the award for excellence in feminist/multicultural scholarship from The New Jersey Project on Inclusive Scholarship, Curriculum and Teaching, and her review of Muse Found in a Colonized Body by Yesenia Montilla was published in *The Rumpus*. This is her first poetry collection.

Dorothy lives by the Jersey Shore with her husband Mark, her black lab Margaret Mary, named for a favorite grammar school nun, and her shepherd-boxer mix, Willow. She used to sing in her church choir but had to retire after admitting to the choirmaster she hadn't been to confession in 40 years.

www.ingramcontent.com/pod-product-compliance
Lightning Source LLC
LaVergne TN
LVHW090539110826
845146LV00003B/1173